Table of Contents

The First Key: Timing
And How It Relates
To Training Your Akita

Timing is your Akita's ability to associate either a positive or a negative outcome with any behavior. Or, more specifically: the result of any behavior.

Since Akitas have limited use of logic and reason, they are unable to associate cause and effect beyond what happens in the immediate present. In other words: Whatever happens as a result of their behavior (good or bad) must happen... pretty much instantaneously.

For example: If your Akita smells the steak you're cooking and jumps up and puts his front paws on your hot stove: your dog's association with the hot stove will be: Stove = hot. (A negative association, that happens instantly).

Yet: If your Akita gets into a 4 lb bag of peanuts and eats them all in a matter of minutes... and an hour later he has painful stomach cramps and diarrhea, then he'll still have no idea that the peanuts caused the stomach pain, because for him: If the result or reaction to his behavior doesn't happen immediately, then his limited logic and reason prevents him from ever learning that 4 lbs of peanuts will cause gastrointestinal distress.

So, it's our responsibility to attach an immediate negative association to eating anything that isn't in his food bowl. Or for any unwanted behavior.

Frequently, Akita owners will ask about behaviors such as "counter surfing" ... where the dog jumps on the kitchen counter to steal a piece of food. Owners wonder how to correct such a behavior, if they're not standing right next to the dog?

And that's where using a bridging technique comes in handy. As soon as your Akita does the unwanted behavior -- even if you're on the other side of the room-- you need to yell, "No, no, no" as you run to him and administer the correction.

By saying "No," right at the moment your Akita does the unwanted behavior, you're creating a virtual snap shot in his mind. And by continuing to say "No! No! No!" as you run to your dog you're forcing him to remember what he is being corrected for.

The studies I've seen suggest that you have (at the most) seven to nine seconds after your Akita exhibits an unwanted behavior... as long as you're using our bridging technique to correct your dog. So, yes; You should be correcting your dog even though he's jumped back off the counter by the time you get to him-- as long as you've said, "No!" right when he first jumped on the counter.

Note: Your verbal correction must always be followed by a leash correction.

Why Consistency
Is Important To Your Akita

The second key is *Consistency*: Pretty much everybody is familiar with the concept of consistency as it relates to dog training. But frequently, Akita owners don't keep it clear in their own head that consistency means your dog perceives the same outcome to a behavior-- every time he does that behavior. And by doing this, we create **a conditioned response.**

Example: While you're getting ready for work, your Akita gets excited and jumps up on you. So, you use one of my techniques to correct that behavior.

Later in the day, you're out talking with a neighbor while your Akita is running around the yard. You're so engrossed in your conversation with your neighbor that you don't realize your dog has come over to you, jumped up and put his front paws on you and now you're scratching him behind his ears-- right where he likes it. And all the while still engrossed in your conversation with your neighbor.

Unfortunately, your Akita will never extinguish this unwanted behavior because he's not receiving clear communication from you. One time he's getting a correction for jumping up. Another time he's getting his ears scratched for jumping up. Your Akita can't tell the difference! In his mind, he's willing to give it "the old college try" because he figures there's at least a 50% chance you'll rub his ears if he jumps up.

Now, you may be asking, "But Adam... what if I want my Akita to jump up on me at certain times?"

Well, the answer to that question is: First you'll need to teach your dog that an unwanted behavior is always unwanted. Unless, of course, we tell him it's okay *first* by issuing a specific command.

But you'll need to be consistent about only letting your Akita jump up when you first tell him it's okay-- and by using a command that is the same,

every time. If your "it's okay to jump up on me" command is "Jump up," …
then you will need to consistently correct your dog if you say any *other*
phrase. For example, try saying the words, "Jelly Bean!" – and patting your
knees. You're still going to correct your dog every time he jumps up...
because you haven't given the "jump up" command, first.

Is this unfair? No. It's completely fair, because you're going to be clear
and consistent about *only* letting him jump up when you've said your "Jump
Up!" command, first. Your dog is smart enough to figure out the difference.
You'll be surprised at how quickly he picks this up.

Motivation And How It Relates To Training Your Akita

The third key is: *Motivation.* Motivation as it relates to Akita training means that: Whatever you do with your dog (either praising him for a desired behavior or correcting him for an unwanted behavior) ... it is done with meaning and gusto!

Have you ever had somebody attempt to compliment you for a job well done... but their compliment was offered in a lethargic tone and without enthusiasm or gusto? Did their compliment make you feel good? Of course not. In my semi-autobiographical book, ***The Dog Training System That Never Fails***, I wrote that a compliment (praise) that lacks any real meaning is what we refer to as being: **not motivational.**

It's the same with a correction. Like my story of the police officer who gives you a ticket for speeding... but the ticket is only for one dollar. For most people, that isn't *motivational enough* to get them to stop speeding. For the police officer's ticket to be motivational to you-- he needs to write a ticket that is going to be expensive enough to get you to adjust your behavior.

Does Your Akita Drive A Corvette?

I like to teach using analogies:

If your Akita could drive, would he drive a shiny red Corvette? Let's pretend he's wealthy and driving a Corvette at 90 mph in a 45 zone. If a police officer gives him a $2 ticket... will that ticket be a motivational correction?

Nope. Not if he's wealthy.

How about a $200,000 ticket? Would that make him stop speeding? You betcha! I don't care how wealthy you are... a $200,000 ticket will make you stop speeding. But there's a problem: It's also going to make you hate cops, hate driving, and hate life in general. You probably won't even want to come out of the house!

So, what does the police officer need to do? He needs to give your dog a nice $200 ticket. Or maybe a $1,000 ticket. But certainly not a $200,000 ticket. And certainly not a $2.

Important --- How motivational to make your praise or your correction will be situational and will depend on how well your Akita understands the exercise.

The first time your Akita successfully does an exercise that you're trying to teach (and you see that proverbial light bulb above his head go on) then you're going to want to make your praise extra motivational. To use the money analogy-- he just won the lottery. But after he's done that same exercise 10 times a day for two years... a simple, "Good dog" will be motivational enough.

The same holds true for a motivational correction. A correction needs to be only motivational enough to get your point across, not more. Of course: A correction for growling at a child will always be a Level 10 ($200,000) correction in contrast to a behavior where the dog makes a simple mistake and the point of the correction is just to communicate to the Akita that he's made a simple mistake. The ability to modulate and moderate our corrections is a concept that is completely lost on the small percentage of the dog training community who advocate a 100% cookie-bribery or so-called, "purely positive" approach to dog training. For some reason, they don't understand that a correction-- a tug on the leash-- can be just a matter of giving your dog feedback. And that not every correction is a Level 10 correction.

As an aside: Many Akitas nip at children but are not what we would consider, "Red Zone" dogs. But they do need a Level 10 correction, since we cannot risk that they ever nip at a child, again. The "purely positive" dog training crowd have no answer for this type of behavior and thus condemn many good dogs to euthanasia.

A Word On Motivation

And How It Relates To
Correcting Aggression:

Think of a numeric scale that goes from zero to positive ten. And then zero to negative ten.

When your Akita is in a calm, resting state-- he is at zero. This is where a balanced dog should always be.

If your Akita is unbalanced and showing ***dominance aggression*** then he is on the positive side of the numeric scale. The closer to positive ten, the more dominant-aggressive he becomes.

When he is showing ***defensive aggression*** then he is on the negative side of the scale. The closer to negative ten, the more defensive aggressive he will become.

If you administer a **motivational** correction when your Akita is showing dominance-aggression, he will become less aggressive. Your goal is to bring him back to zero. However-- if your correction **is not motivational**, then he will show more of the dominance aggressive.

With defensive aggression, it's even more tricky: If you over-correct your Akita, he will become more defensive. With defensive aggression, the secret is to give just enough of a correction to get your point across and then let the dog settle down. Further corrections will typically make your dog more defensive and undermine trust.

You can usually tell the difference between these two types of aggression because of the context the behavior displayed itself around and also by watching your Akita's ears: Forward, upright ears typically indicate dominance whereas lower, folded-back ears indicate defensive aggression.

Why We Correct Our Akitas But Never Punish Our Akitas

It is the nature of all animals to do more of behaviors that give them pleasure and do less behaviors that cause displeasure. We recognize this basic premise and uses it to our advantage, whereas other approaches choose to ignore it.

The sooner you are able to convince your Akita that choosing to do what you want him to do brings him pleasure (and the opposite brings him displeasure) ... then you're on the road to getting amazing results.

To be clear: We are dog lovers. So, when we talk about "displeasure" ... we are **_not_** talking about hitting, inflicting damage, injuring or suffering humiliation upon our dogs. There is a huge difference between correcting behaviors and punishing our dogs. ***You should not punish your Akita--*** because dogs do not have the capacity to do things out of malice. Instead, we correct unwanted behavior and teach dogs that the sooner they do what we want, the sooner they will receive pleasure in their life and eliminate displeasure in their life.

You'll learn in the coming pages that your dog is smart enough to figure out the difference.

Equipment You'll Need
To Train Your Akita

Just like a cobbler needs certain tools to make shoes and a carpenter needs his hammer and saw to build a house, so does the professional dog trainer or amateur Akita owner to get maximum results in minimal time.

The main tools you'll need for teaching your dog (in no particular order) are:

- A 6' Leather Dog Leash

- A Buckle Collar

- A Prong Collar (also called a "pinch collar") ** If you live in Australia, New Zealand or the UK, you may need to buy the Starmark "Good Dog" collar instead. This is a plastic version of the prong collar. Why? Because the inmates (the cookie-pusher trainers) are running the asylum when it comes to dog training.

- A 30' long line.

- A 1' tab leash (Typically referred to as just a: "Tab")

- Optional: A Remote electronic collar (e-collar)

You may have already formed opinions about some of these training tools. Some readers may even be crinkling their nose, already.

But wait!

Please allow me to explain and I'll go into more detail about how each of these tools work and why they are the most humane way to train your Akita.

The 6 Foot Leather Leash

The best leash to use is a 6 foot leather leash. Although lately I've been using leashes made of nylon webbing, since we now live in a desert climate that has a tendency to dry out leather too quickly. Regardless, you'll want a 6' leash not a 4' or 10' leash.

You'll also want the type with a regular harness snap on one end-- preferably with the snap braided and stitched to the leash, although some of the finer Amish leashes are just braided and those are of great quality, too.

Leather leashes are what all of the really good trainers use. Sure, you can use the polypropylene or nylon leashes. But nothing beats supple leather in your hands when you're working with a leash for hours a week. It's the difference between wearing leather shoes and wearing nylon shoes.

The One-Foot Tab Leash

The "Tab" is a one foot leash we make our Akitas wear, both around the house and when we're in an "off-leash" setting. You cannot give a motivational correction without having at least a tab attached to your dog's training collar. (Simply grabbing the chain part of the training collar doesn't work!)

You can buy a tab leash from any of the big box pet stores (or online). They typically cost around $8.

For a more economical alternative, you can make your own tab by buying a short piece of soft rope at your local hardware store and attaching it to a $0.35 harness snap. I usually just run the rope through the loop end of the harness snap and then tie the two ends of the rope together with a knot. Really, you just need something that gives you enough length so that you can get a bit of slack when you tug on it.

The Buckle Collar

The plain leather buckle collar is the one your dog will wear at most times, but it typically isn't used in a training context. You can use it to attach your Akita's identification tags or if you're using a remote electronic collar-- the buckle collar will be what you attach your leash to-- as the leash really isn't used as anything more than something you can grab onto if the unexpected (like a car) suddenly appears and you don't yet have enough control over your Akita to be comfortable with him "off leash."

Many owners prefer the rolled leather buckle collar as it doesn't leave an indent in the coat.

The Slip Collar or "Choke Chain" Collar

Before the prong collar was developed (see below) pretty much everybody used the slip collar (a piece of fine rope with a metal ring on each end) or it's metal counterpart, the "choke chain."

The slip collar and the choke chain are identical tools-- but one is made of fabric and the other is made of chain link.

I have no idea why it came to be called a choke chain, as the only way it can choke your dog is if it's misused. And if we're going to start calling things by names based on how they're not supposed to be used, then we might as well start calling cake: "Fat Makers".

The slip collar is looped one end into the other, just like you would a slip knot. While facing the dog, you'll want to make it look like a "P" as you put it over your Akita's head. This is because we typically work with our dogs on our left side, and putting it on this way will allow the ring to slide and relax after you've given a tug-and-release on the leash. If you put the slip collar on the dog the opposite way– it will stay tight, even when you relax the leash.

The problem with the choke chain is that you have to give more of a physical tug on the leash to get a motivational correction than you do with a prong collar. The prong collar is more like power steering on a car.

So, if you don't have access to a prong collar (or you're attending a dog event where they (gasp!) won't let you use a prong collar because they're uninformed or too easily swayed by political correctness – then the choke chain is a decent substitute, but not one I immediately reach for when training a Akita.

The Prong Collar-- also known as the Pinch Collar

Yes... it looks like a medieval torture device. But looks can be deceiving. It's actually one of the safest and most humane dog training collars you can use.

"Don't Judge A Book By It's Cover"

The prong collar is designed to replicate the way the mother would correct her puppies. Or similarly, how the Alpha dog in a pack would correct the subordinate dogs... by giving them a "nip" on the neck.

The prong collar (also frequently called: a pinch collar) is made of a series of prongs that link together.

Most prong collars are designed pretty much the same way: There is a safety ring that rides next to your dog's neck and a "D" shaped ring that you hook your leash onto. Some prong collar manufacturers have developed a "quick release" mechanisms that may work somewhat differently.

A Safe Fit For The Prong Collar

In order to properly size and fit the collar, you must do the following:

1.) Understand that size and fit *are two different issues.* The size is determined by the size of the prong... not the diameter of the whole collar. Sizes usually come in small, medium and large. Once you have to use more than eight prongs, you'll want to upgrade to the next size prong collar in most cases, although some more sensitive individual Akitas may work well on a smaller size prong.

2.) The fit of the collar is determined by adding or subtracting prongs to change the diameter. Simply break the collar open at one of the looser prongs <u>in the middle</u> of the collar and pop off one or more of the individual prongs.

3.) Properly fitted, you should only be able to fit approximately ½ to one finger space between the tip of the prong and the skin of your Akita's neck. Trust me, you won't be doing your dog any favor if it's too loose and you have to give 10 times the number of corrections and it's rubbing and chafing her neck because <u>YOU</u> weren't using it correctly. Make sure it's a snug fit... ½ to one finger space!!!

The trick to putting the prong collar on correctly is that you'll need to break the collar apart in the middle-- by unsnapping two of the prongs, and then put it around your Akita's neck. If you just try to slide it over your dog's head, then you've fitted the collar way, way too loose.

Don't Get Collar-Smart
With Me!

To reiterate: If you ONLY put the training collar on your Akita immediately before training, she'll become collar-smart. She'll respond like a complete angel when the collar is on but like a real devil when the collar is off. So, just like the Alpha dog who always has the ability to correct the subordinate dogs (with her mouth)... so must you! In other words, leave the collar and tab (1 foot leash) on your dog *any time you're interacting with her*. And take it off at night or when you leave her unsupervised.

You'll know when she's proofed when you can bet me $100 that your Akita is responding with 100% reliability. If you take the prong collar off sooner, you're running the risk of making her collar-smart!

The prong collar is like power steering. It is a phenomenal tool for teaching your Akita to walk on a loose leash as well as allowing you to give your dog a motivational correction in a manner that gets your point across. (No pun intended). Used by anyone other than a complete idiot, this training collar is safe and humane.

More "real world" professional trainers use the prong collar more than probably any other training collar on the market, today.

The Long Line

Before training became so commercialized, we used to just go down to the local hardware store and buy a 30 foot length of soft rope for about a dollar and a harness snap for $0.25 cents.

Today, you can buy a long line pre-cut from most of the big box pet stores.

Your long line should be strong enough that it will stop your Akita from running while at full gallop and light enough that it doesn't impede his movement (although dragging the line will almost always take some getting used to for a new dog).

But the most important feature of your long line is that it is thick and tactile enough that it won't slip out from underneath your boot (especially when wet!) if your Akita starts to run off.

The Remote Collar

(From Wikipedia) *"The [remote electronic] collar produces a static pulse stimulation at varying degrees of intensity and duration to the dog via a small transmitter incorporated into a dog collar. Some collar models also include a tone or vibrational setting, as an alternative to or in conjunction with the static pulse stimulation. Others include integration with Internet mapping capabilities and GPS to locate canines or alert owners of their whereabouts.*

Originally used in the late 1960s to train hunting dogs, early collars were very high powered. Electronic collars are now readily available and have been applied to a wide range of purposes, including behavioral modification, anti-theft and GPS location and tracking, obedience training, and pet containment, as well as military, police and service training. While similar systems are available for other animals, the most common are the collars designed for domestic dogs.

Electronic collars may be used in conjunction with positive reinforcement and / or utilizing other principles of operant conditioning, depending on the trainer's methods[2] either as a form of positive punishment, where the stimulation is applied at the moment an undesired behavior occurs, in order to reduce the frequency of that behavior; or as a form of negative reinforcement, where a continuous stimulation is applied until the moment a desired behavior occurs, in order to increase the frequency of that behavior.

Some trainers use a low level of electrical stimulation as a marker and pair it with a reward, making the collar a conditioned re-enforcer, similar to clicker training. Some electronic collars include vibration or tone-only settings, which can be used as a "neutral stimulus" for most dogs. A special application exists for the positive reinforcement and marker training of deaf dogs. This happens when the training is to "pair the mild stimulation produced by the collar with food and other rewards.

As a consequence, the stimulation can then be used to reinforce desirable behaviors conditionally in much the same manner as applying other common conditioned re-enforcers (e.g. "Good")." (Lindsay 2000, p. 136) Some professional dog trainers have a rigorous science-based understanding and education in canine learning, behavioral therapy and canine temperament and have mastered the technical and timing application of electronic collars to number behavioral or training goals. They advocate the successful operation and usage of electronic collars through the guidance of a professional who specializes in these types of devices and its various applications in applied animal behavioral therapy or various dog training. As with any dog training tool, improper usage, abuse, inadequate application and negligence can create undesirable results."

The remote electronic collar (from here forward referred to as an "e-collar") is similar to a tens machine in a chiropractic office. While technically it delivers an electrical "shock" – the sensation is more akin to a mild vibration than it is to a static electrical shock. (Not to be confused with e-collars that only vibrate, since "vibration collars" are not adjustable and therefore have no way to be adjusted to match your Akita's motivation level).

The e-collar, in contrast, can be adjusted to vary the intensity of this stimulation, depending on your Akita's distraction level-- similar to the way a child will not hear you talking to him while he's playing a video game.

I could write a whole book on just e-collar training and some day I probably will. But here I'll just summarize the use of the e-collar:

First, I'll introduce the e-collar to a Akita by putting

the stimulation level to the lowest setting that the dog can barely feel-- and then simply walk backwards while "tapping" on the button. As the dog makes an effort to move toward me, I'll stop tapping. When he gets distracted again, I'll back away at a different angle and continue tapping until he chooses to stop the tapping by turning and moving toward me.

The best analogy I've heard for explaining this concept was from Robin MacFarlaine, an e-collar instructor who owns "That's My Dog!" in Dubuque, Iowa. Robin compares this exercise to what her young daughter does when Robin is trying to watch a movie: "Mom. Mom. Mom. Mom." ... until Robin can no longer focus on the movie and must pay attention to the child. It's a nagging of sorts, and the dog learns to shut it off by paying attention. (The byproduct is also that your dog discovers that you-- the handler-- is more fun than anything else, too!)

If the Akita I'm working with still doesn't understand, I'll use a light tug on the leash to direct him to come toward me and tap the button at the same time.

Once I've practiced this attention exercise in a variety of different locations and the Akita I'm training is now comfortable with the e-collar, I'll start to blend the "e-stim" with my leash corrections for the other exercises later in this book; first on-leash and then later off leash.

The Starmark
"Good Dog" Collar

A dog trainer friend in New Zealand sent me a letter asking what I'd recommend for teaching a disabled client how to work with their soft-temperament Akita? Unfortunately, New Zealand has banned the use of remote electronic collars-- despite the fact that they've been proven time and again to be safe, humane and effective if used properly. They've caved to the cookie-bribery extremists who choose to think more with their emotions and junk science than with logic or reason.

My response to this trainer in New Zealand is as follows:

*"I'd probably recommend going with the "**Starmark Good Dog collar**" (a plastic pinch collar replica) instead of the metal pinch collar, if you're in New Zealand. With the metal one, I'd be too worried that customs would seize it [as I'm under the impression they don't allow pinch collars, either]. Maybe you could order a quantity of 10 and resell them to other clients or other professional dog trainers? You might be able to negotiate a discount, too!"*

"As for your disabled client: I'm not clear as to what specifically is his disability? It's really a shame that the New Zealand government takes such a ludditian stance on e-collars. This would be as perfect an example of when an e-collar would be beneficial as I could possibly think of. For a disabled client, the trainer (you) would first teach the dog the commands and that the e-collar is a replacement for the leash correction. Then, once the dog understands, it would be very easy to transfer it over to the owner-- as all they'd need to do (for the most part) is issue a clear command and then press the button to reinforce the command."

"Without the e-collar, I'd recommend you do a board-and-train with the dog. Get the dog 100% responding to off-leash voice commands. Then, bring the owner into the picture. The owner will still occasionally need to use the leash and collar to reinforce the commands-- because

occasionally, the dog will test the owner (as I'm sure you know). "

R-E-S-P-E-C-T: Establishing A Proper Relationship Between You And Your Akita

In order for your Akita to begin learning anything... you must first establish yourself as the pack leader.

In every relationship – whether human or dog-- there will be one that is more dominant and one that is less dominant. Two dominant animals can co-exist together, as long as there is not a conflict. But life is full of conflicts. So, sooner or later there will eventually be a conflict; I want to go right and you want to go left or if I want to play with this toy by myself and so do you... there will be conflict.

As humans, we can use higher level communication, negotiation and logic and reason to settle our differences. But dogs don't have this ability.

Once there is conflict, the more dominant animal will eventually emerge. In the context of the pet/owner relationship: The winner of that conflict must be you.

With humans, it's different. I can be dominant in one situation and you can be dominant in another situation and we can coexist peacefully if we both agree that the other has more pressing needs. We're able to do this, because as humans we possess higher logic and reason. But with dogs, it's different. If a subordinate dog wants to act dominant-- it's only because the truly dominant dog is letting him do that.

Until he doesn't.

Now-- does that mean you need to win every conflict and make every decision for your Akita?

No, of course not. Just the high-value ones.

Nothing In Life Is Free

In the beginning, you'll need to exercise your role as the pack leader by making most of the low value decisions for your Akita. Because he's not listening to you and thus assumes for himself that he is the dominant one in the relationship-- we'll need to re-establish your relationship with your Akita into a more positive, balanced and healthy way. And we do that by adopting a "Nothing In Life Is Free" (NILIF) attitude.

A lot has been written on the internet about "Nothing In Life Is Free" as a dog training approach. There are many variations of it, depending on who you talk with. But I'll outline my approach to "Nothing In Life Is Free" below:

If you own a dominant dog then you'll need to follow these guidelines, at least until you establish which one of you (hint: You!) is the pack leader. NILIF will help create a more natural relationship between you and your Akita.

But don't be fooled: This approach also works on shy, timid Akitas– because the shy, timid dog gains confidence by knowing that you are a strong leader who will protect and keep him safe.

Following our Nothing In Life Is Free: Alpha Dog Boot Camp approach will create a balanced, harmonious and more natural relationship between you and your dog.

Remember: Akitas are not "hairy children." They have different drives and instincts than children do. And although there are some similarities– your dog will interpret your behavior through the eyes of canine genetics that have evolved over several hundred years of domestication.

1. Neuter or spay your Akita. Not only will it eliminate the possibility for various types of cancer developing, but it will also reduce hormonal dominance levels. Have your veterinarian give your dog a full health check-up.

2. Stop roughhousing and playing tug-of-war games with your Akita. It teaches your dog that challenging you is fun. It is not a productive activity in any manner, for the dominant dog. When your dog wins he thinks he is stronger than you; and stronger dogs are always higher in the social hierarchy of the pack.

3. Teach your Akita the down-stay exercise and use it throughout your day. Instead of letting your dog wander around the house or go where he pleases, make him hold a down-stay while you're preparing dinner, watching television, changing your clothes, etc… Make your dog stay down for at least a full 30 minutes every day.

4. Do not reward your Akita if he hasn't first earned the praise. That is, make him "work for the praise." If your dog approaches you and demands to be petted, make him sit first. Or hold a down-stay. Or some other exercise. He needs to learn that **nothing in life is free!**

5. Only issue commands that you are in a position to enforce. In other words, don't use the formal "Come" command if you're not in a position to physically make your Akita come. Do not tell your dog, "Down" if he's not wearing a training collar and short leash (tab). Otherwise you'll be teaching your dog that your commands are meaningless. And in the pack, when the alpha dog wants a subordinate dog to do something… he's never ignored, as this would jeopardize the survival of the pack.

6. Don't wait to see if your Akita will obey a command. If you're having dominance problems with your dog, then every command needs to be enforced, immediately. Eventually, your dog will become conditioned to respond to commands– and at that same time, you will have noticed your dog has begun to see you as his pack leader. But until that point (which can take several months) … you need to enforce commands as soon as you give them.

7. There's an old military slogan: Lead, Follow or Get out of the Way. In short: You need to be the leader. This means that you need to be the first one to walk through doors, the first to eat, and the first to decide where you're going to walk. Alpha dogs never walk behind the pack. They always lead. If your Akita is pulling on the leash or walking out in front of you– you need to change this and learn how to get your Akita to walk on a loose leash and pay

more attention to you than anything else that may be going on.

8. Your Akita needs to "work" for everything. Does he want you to throw the ball? Then he needs to lay down first. Is he hungry? Then he needs to sit and stay there, until you tell him that it's okay to eat.

9. Your Akita should be wearing a leash and training collar, anytime you're with him. You cannot enforce a command if your dog isn't wearing a short leash (a tab) and a training collar.

10. If your Akita is not wearing a leash and training collar, then he needs to be confined in his crate or dog run. Free run of the house is no longer permitted. Seems harsh? Only to us humans. Remember: You're dealing with a dominant dog. Act like the pack leader so he'll view you as the pack leader! Note: Never leave a training collar on your dog when he's unsupervised– even in the crate or kennel run.

11. You can create your own short leash (tab) by buying a short piece of rope (or plastic coated cable if your Akita is a chewer) and then tie a knot at the end of the rope. Attach the other end to a harness snap (about .37 cents $USD at your local hardware store). It just needs to be long enough that you can grab, create a bit of slack, and give a tug on the tab when you're correcting your dog for bad behavior.

12. Do not let your Akita sleep on the bed. And do not let your dog sleep on your child's bed. This is very important. More dominance and aggression problems are created by people who let their dogs sleep on their bed than probably any other single behavior. The pack leader always sleeps on higher ground. Subordinate dogs sleep on lower ground. Being higher (or on top) is a dominance behavior.

13. Work short obedience sessions, throughout the day. 5-15 minutes. There is no limit as to how many obedience sessions you can work with your Akita. The more, the better.

14. When your Akita does something right, praise him. The way to effectively praise your dog is by saying, "Good dog!" and then making physical contact. Dogs are very physical animals. And don't be shy: Some

Akitas like to be patted while others like to be stroked. Observe which style of praise your dog likes best, but always make physical contact when you praise your dog.

15. Correct your Akita every time your dog exhibits an unwanted behavior. There are many different ways to correct your dog. Remember: You must make sure that your dog gets corrected every time he exhibits an unwanted behavior, until he drops that behavior. (See point 10, above).

16. Akitas live in the moment. You should, too. If your dog exhibits a bad behavior, correct him for it and then forget it. It's not personal. Dogs don't do things out of "spite." They do not possess the ability to use long term and higher logic.

17. You decide when your Akita is allowed to meet visitors. Do not let your dog immediately run up to visitors and greet them. You need to decide when and how– which in most cases, should be after holding a sit-stay or down-stay.

Here's Why You Need To
Teach Your Akita To Pay Attention To You, First!

Before teaching your Akita any of the other commands, you'll need to first teach him to pay attention to you. Sound like a good idea?

The exercise you'll use is called, the "Attention Getter."

This exercise teaches your Akita two fundamental lessons (for the price of one!):

1. To walk on a loose leash without pulling.

2. To pay more attention to you than to anything else that's going on. (Including tennis balls, cats, other animals, food, etc...)

You'll need to first properly fit your prong collar and grab your leather six-foot leash.

Hold your six-foot leash at about 1/3 of the way down and with two hands, pretend to glue it to your crotch region as if you were connecting your hands and the leash to your belt buckle. As soon as the dog starts to run forward, you need to do a sharp right-about face turn, and RUN the opposite direction... before your dog hits the end of the leash.

Your Akita will automatically receive a sharp snap when he hits the end. You need to do this exercise as you walk back and forth, and within about two minutes he will realize that if he stays close to you, he avoids getting left out to hit the end of the leash. If he chooses to ignore you, then you teach him that you're not just going to stand there like a stationary pole or a tree but rather you're going to "get out of Dodge" by running the other way.

If your Akita runs out ahead of you to the north, you'll turn and go south. If he runs ahead of you to the south, you'll go north.

When your Akita starts staying with you, praise him. Reach down and touch him... but keep moving! Soon, your dog will learn that it's really his choice: If he wants to, he can go all day and get nothing but praise. He also learns that you are a more immediate concern than any of the other distractions.

The prong collar will make your corrections motivational. If when your dog hits the end of the leash he doesn't feel uncomfortable.... there's absolutely no reason for your dog to stop doing it. The prong collar makes this exercise easy-- just remember that your leash should be slack almost all of the time and only tight momentarily when he hits the end of the leash.

This exercise is not done by tugging on the leash with your arms. Your Akita will correct himself since your feet are moving in the opposite direction and he's choosing not to move in that direction *with you.*

The "Take A Break" Command

The "Take a break" command is a simple way to teach your Akita that the exercise (any exercise) is finished and he can, "take five."

I'm going to explain this now, before I teach you the individual exercises, because it's important that you teach it in conjunction with each behavior.

The reason this command is important is because it replaces the "stay" command. Stay is actually a double command. When you think about it, there's not time when you would ever tell your dog to, "Sit!" and then he would immediately be allowed to get right back up. So, of course he should stay. **Stay is implicit in the command.** With my system, your dog learns to continue doing the command until you tell him, "Take a break!" This means you don't have to give double or triple commands such as, "Stay!" "Wait!" "Don't get up!" or "Stay! Stay! Stay! Stay!"

Your Akita learns to listen and respond to a command when you say it once-- and to hold that position until you return and tell him, "Take a break."

To teach the, "Take a break!" command, we usually start by teaching the dog the place command, first (see below). But really, any stationary command will do.

When you're ready to tell your Akita that it's okay to get up-- tell him, "Take a break!" and then use a little bit of touch and motion to indicate it's okay for him to break the command. He might be a little unsure at first, but once he gets up-- lavish praise on him.

He'll soon start to wait for the, "Take a break" command because he will learn very quickly that if he breaks the command/position before you say, "Take a break!" he will receive a correction. But if instead he waits for the, "Take a break!" command-- he'll get all the praise and love for having listened. You'll be truly surprised at how quickly your Akita will figure this out.

Teaching Your Akita To Come, Every Time You Call

Step 1

Start by taking your Akita to the same types of places where you'll want him to ultimately be off-leash. But let him wear the long line. That's right... just let him drag it around.

Initially, he may be a bit bothered by it. Many Akitas will step on the long line accidentally and may even mildly self-correct. Don't worry about it... your dog will get over it. After a couple of days, he'll forget that he's dragging the extra 15-30 feet of line around.

And when you see that happen, then you will be like the Alpha (the strongest and fastest in the pack) in the sense that you'll always be able to step on the end of that long line and make him come back to you.

Step 2

Before you call your Akita, nonchalantly grab the long line at a random length, but with only enough slack in the line that running backwards five feet or less will make it tight.

Tell your Akita, "Come!" and then run backwards and give a tug on the long line... as you're moving away from him. After you tug on the long line, drop it on the ground. *Do not reel the long line back in.*

As your dog starts to run toward you, give him verbal praise. "Goooood boy!!!"

Do not bend forward, as a forward posture will be communicating with body language in a way that suggests you're "pushing" him away. Instead, lean backwards, as leaning back is inviting body language. You'll be surprised at how just a little change in body language will make it easier for your Akita to understand what you're asking him to do.

If your Akita stops half way to you... or he gets distracted, then walk all the way to him and grab the line short, as if he was wearing his one-foot tab. Reissue your "Come!" command and then tug-and-release as you quickly walk backwards (bringing him with you) to the same spot where you originally stood, when you first called him.

Your correction should be a firm tug-and-release.

Then, try it again.

If your dog runs after a cat or another dog, call out your "Come," command a second or two before he hits the end of the line and self-corrects.

As he turns toward you to see what happened, you'll be walking backwards away from him to encourage him to come in to you. As he makes any effort to move toward you-- *praise him and continue praising him as he comes back to you.*

Another exercise is to tie the long line to one end of a tree, place your dog on a down-stay toward the end of the long line, and then walk to the other side of the tree. So, if you're working with a thirty foot long line, you'll now effectively be working just under sixty feet away from your dog.

If your Akita sees a bird and runs away from you, you'll say, "No!" and then when he hits the end of the long line, he'll think you were able to correct him from sixty feet away.

Note: A common rookie mistake is to simply reissue the command and then reel your Akita in, hand-over-hand without going to your dog. This doesn't work and it teaches your dog to be "leash smart". One of the secrets to working with the long line is that: *What your Akita feels on the end of the line should be pretty much the same as what he feels when he's wearing the tab.*

If, when you go to correct your Akita, he runs away: Say, "No!" and step on the long line.

When he hits the end of the line, he will self-correct. Then go all the way to him and reissue your verbal correction: "No!" and give him a firm tug-and-release -- just like if he was wearing the tab. Then, reissue the, "Come" command. In effect: You're teaching two things. First, that running away from you is unacceptable. And second: When I say, "Come," you need to be moving toward me.

Do this enough times and your Akita will learn that it's impossible to run away from you, and he'll stop trying.

Step 3

If you practice in a variety of settings and around a variety of distractions, after a few weeks your Akita will start being reliable. Do not be fooled into thinking that just because your dog is responding reliably to you in your front yard, that he will respond the same way, at the park. You need to reinforce the exercise in a variety of different types of locations. I usually like to work in: A park setting; A parking lot setting; A residential area; and a commercial area.

After you work with your dog in a variety of different settings with the long line, he'll start to extrapolate the exercise.

Step 4

Now, do the same thing... except focus on working your dog around different types of distractions, rather than just different locations. I don't typically like dog parks, but they can be useful in teaching your dog to come around lots of distractions at once: Tennis balls, other dogs and crazy people.

The more creative you can get with the type of distractions, the better your Akita will get. (Think: Chickens, goats, kids playing catch with a football, etc...)

Step 5

At this point, you can put your Akita in a small enclosed area (like a small residential yard) and substitute the long line for the tab. Everything about how you now work with your dog should be exactly the same as when you were using the long line. The reason this works is because: The species has limited reason and logic.

If you see that your Akita is responding reliably, then you're ready to progress to taking him anywhere with you and can be confident that your dog will respond, off-leash.

A Note Of Caution: With all training, we're building a conditioned response. However-- reinforcement is forever! So, if you begin to see that your Akita's response time begins to slip (for example: If it takes a double or triple command before he decides to obey the recall command) then use that response as your indication that you need to take a step backwards and reinforce his conditioning by going back to the long line or "setting him up" by working with him in a small yard so that you can go to him and correct him the first time you issue the command. This way you'll be able to maintain peak performance.

Training Your Akita
To Sit And Stay

There are two ways to teach your Akita to sit and stay.

Remember: The "stay" part of the command is implicit. There's absolutely no time when you will tell your dog to, "sit!" and he would be allowed to immediately get back up again. I.E., He should remain sitting until you tell him, "Take a break!"

In other words, the "stay!" command is redundant. There's no need to say, "Stay... wait... don't get up..." etc. Simply tell your Akita to sit and when he sits, then praise him.

The first and most common way to teach your Akita to go into the sit position is to begin with the leash in your right hand. Hold it short, but so that the snap that is attached to your dog's collar is loose (hanging straight down).

Now, tell your Akita, "Sit!" and give a tug straight up toward the ceiling. (A tug means that the leash is tight for only ¼ of a second-- and then becomes slack again). At the same time that you tug, push down on the dog's rear end.

The upward tug and the downward push on his rump should happen at the same time. If your Akita doesn't want to drop his tush to the ground, slide your hand down around the backside of his rear elbows and his rear legs should collapse him into the sit-position.

Rinse and repeat several times, gradually applying less downward pressure with your left hand. So, as the dog begins to associate the word, "Sit!" with the behavior, the association will also link with the upward tug on the leash.

The second way to teach your Akita to go into the sit position is identical to what I've described above-- except that you'll be palming a cookie in your

RIGHT HAND.

Say, "Sit!" and <u>then</u> tug upward on the leash with your right hand and push downward with your left. Except that this time, when you relax the leash with your right hand (the one with the cookie in it) you'll drop your hand down in front of your dog's nose and use the cookie to lure him into position.

After several repetitions, you'll want to phase the cookie out, as you see your dog begin to associate the word, "sit" with the behavior.

As for the stay part of this exercise: Pretend your dog is sitting on one spot. If he gets up, tell him, "sit!" and correct him back into the sit-position.

He needs to wait until you tell him, "Take a break!" As I mentioned earlier, "Take a break" tells your dog that the exercise is finished and it's okay for him to get up. Make it fun! Jump around. If he doesn't understand, it's okay to pull gently on the leash and bring him out of position-- and then praise profusely.

Next, put your Akita back into the sit position. Walk away. If he gets up and walks away from the spot where you made him sit, you'll want to say, "No!" as soon as he gets up. Then firmly say, "No! No! No!" as you walk back to him, pick up the leash and then say, "No!" (and tug on the leash) as you walk him back to the same spot where you originally had him sit.

No praise, since he just broke the command.

Next, walk away again. If he stays in his spot, walk back and praise him-- then give him a, "Take a break!"

You'll want to practice in a variety of different locations and with a variety of different distractions in order to proof your Akita. The more creative you get with your distractions, the more reliable your dog will become.

How To Teach
The Down-Stay Command

Once the sit-stay command has been taught, the next step is to teach your Akita to lie down on command.

To go into the down position, you'll want to start with your dog sitting in the heel position. I.E., On your left side.

Next, grab the leash about one-foot down from the snap with your right hand. Place your left hand on your dog's back-- just behind the shoulder bones. That spot is a pressure point.

Now, tell your Akita, "Down!" and then tug and release on the leash with your right hand *and at the same time* rock to the side and push down *with your left hand.* Your dog's front legs should collapse under him.

Some Akitas can get very resistant about being placed into the down position because it is a submissive position. If you encounter resistance, palm a cookie and press your hand with the cookie in it toward your dog's nose and then lure him downward. You should push into the dog's nose and then drop your hand down so that your knuckles are touching the ground. Your dog's nose will follow. At the same time, use your left-hand on his back, exactly as described above and rock him into the down position.

After a few repetitions, he'll realize you're not trying to dominate him-- you're just putting him into a down position. Start associating the leash tug at this point and then following with the cookie once he's in position.

Once he shows you that he's beginning to understand, phase out the cookie. At this point, you'll still be pushing and rocking on that pressure point behind his shoulder bones with your left hand and tugging on the leash with your right hand.

As he starts to understand, you'll gradually go through the following transition:

1. Saying the command, "Down!" and then bending over and touching your dog on the back with your left hand while tugging downward on the leash with your right hand.

2. Saying the command, "Down!" but no longer touching your Akita's back with your left hand, but still bending over and tugging in a downward direction with your right hand.

3. Saying the command, "Down!" and only bending half-way, yet still tugging in a downward direction.

4. Standing straight up without bending over, saying the command, "Down!" and giving a forward tug-and-release on the leash.

At this point, you should be able to begin issuing the down command from various angles and directions. I.E., Mix it up! Don't always stand in front of your Akita at the same angle when you issue the command.

Of course, the "stay" component of the exercise is implicit in the command, "Down!" Just like the, "Sit!" command, there is no time when your Akita would be allowed to immediately get back up... so of course he should stay in that position. When you're ready for your dog to get up, then you'll issue the your, "Take a break!" command and with a gentle pull on the leash, a little touch and a little motion-- you're telling your dog that the exercise is finished.

Frequently, when you've just taught your Akita the down-stay command... but when you bend over to praise her, she rolls on her back. What should you do?

Here's what you'll need to do: Take a step backwards. Literally.

Did your Akita roll right-side up? Just give verbal praise.

Did she stay on his back? Then walk to the end of the leash.

Did she roll right-side up, and then stand up? Step in and reissue the down command, with a downward tug and release of the leash.

Block her from creeping forward with her body. Your goal is to teach her to go down and stay down on the same spot where you initially gave the command.

What if she stayed on her back? Then (while still standing at the end of your 6′ leash) pull with constant tension toward you… even if you have to drag her forward a little. It's okay to repeat the down-command. Release the tension as she starts to roll, right-side up.

Now practice walking into your dog and leaning over to give physical praise: Start by just touching her head. If she starts to roll submissive when you bend over to touch her, then stand up straight again. Your goal is to communicate that rolling over makes the praise "go away".

DPTrainer4 on our DogProblems.com discussion forum adds: "Down can be a difficult command for many Akitas simply because it is a submissive position."

"My current dog is one that likes to 'cockroach' (a very technical term, you see) rolling onto her side and back at any given opportunity. Teaching the down was somewhat difficult."

"The way I corrected this was to teach the down while she was in a heel position. I would have her lay down, then the moment she cockroached, I was off into a 'Heel,' and if she was not right behind me (which is entirely possible) she self-corrected. She learned to stay in the sphinx position rather quickly."

DPTrainer5 on our DogProblems.com discussion forum offers the following input: "It is quite possible that you or perhaps a family member or friend is unknowingly reinforcing the rolling over in times other than training sessions. For example, your friend comes over to your house, greets your dog and she automatically "cockroaches" and the person might say something like, "Awww. She's so cute. She wants her belly rubbed." Then they rub your dog's belly, thus reinforcing the rolling over. I suggest not petting your dog at all while she's on her back. That may help during training because your dog will not have been rewarded for the behavior at other times."

Teaching Your Akita
The "Place" Command

The "Place" command is one of the easiest yet most impressive exercises you can teach your Akita.

It's basically a way to tell your Akita to climb up on something (his bed or pillow for example) and stay there. This allows you to have your dog be part of the action without being the center of attention. For example, if you have a dinner party, you'll no longer have to lock your dog up in his crate or in a back room. Simply put him on a, "place" command and he'll stay there until you give him the, "Take a break!" command.

First, pick an object for your Akita to "place" on. This can be a plastic top from a tote (box). Or a heavy beach towel folded in half. Or even your dog's bed or pillow. Really, anything will work as long as the edges are easily distinguishable to your dog. We like to use an elevated cot or a Kuranda bed. Whatever we're using, we'll call it a "place board".

Here's how to teach the place command:

Stand with your dog next to the place board.

Tell your Akita, "Place!" and then pull on the leash toward the place board. It's important that you're pulling in a directional manner, not straight up toward the ceiling-- so that your leash relaxes when your dog moves in that direction.

The concept is: Pressure on/Pressure off. Keep constant tension on the leash until your Akita makes an effort to get on the place board. As soon as he does, immediately relax the leash.

Imagine it this way: Once you say the command, "Place!" the ground becomes fire and the safe zone is being on the place board. So, it's your job to get your baby's feet off the fire as quickly as possible. Pretend to act very urgently about it, and this will produce a fast response from your Akita.

Remember to relax the leash (no tension) once all four of your dog's feet are up on the place board and immediately lavish praise.

Now, take a step backwards. If your dog steps off the place board, immediately step back in and say, "Place!" and pull the leash tight-- relaxing it only when he's back on the place board.

This is one of the few exercises where you're *not* giving a tug-and-release on the leash but rather a constant pull.

Note: Do not lift your Akita up while you're getting him onto the place board. Pull in a directional/horizontal manner so that he steps up onto the place board himself, then relax the leash when all four feet are no longer on the floor.

When your Akita has stayed on the place board for a few moments, give him a, "Take a break!" command so that he knows it's okay to get up. Gradually build the amount of time that he stays on the place command by practicing this exercise while you're eating breakfast, preparing meals, watching television, etc...

How To Teach
Your Akita To "Heel"

The heel command can mean one of two things:

First, it's a command of motion. It means: Walk along side me. Since motion is fun and positive to your Akita, it's okay to use your dog's name in conjunction with the "heel" command. For example: "Banjo, heel!" because we want to associate positive things with your dog's name. (It should stand to reason that you should try to avoid using your dog's name and the, "No!" command if at all possible).

And second, the heel command is a positional command that requires your Akita to be lined up so that his right leg is parallel to *your left leg*. Your toes and his toes should be lined up along the same axis when you're standing still.

For a basic heel command, your dog should already know the "Attention-getter" exercise described earlier in this book.

Remember: The Attention-getter only had two objectives: 1. Get 51% of your Akita's attention on you. 2. To keep a loose leash so that your leash looks like the letter "J".

But the, "Heel" command takes it one step further by teaching your Akita to do everything he learned with the attention-getter exercise... but to also stay in position on your left hand side.

Now, when you begin walking, tell your Akita, "Heel". If he's already in the heel position, reach down and praise him and continue praising him for a few steps... then give him the, "Take a break!" command so that he knows that the exercise is finished and it's okay for him to leave the heel position.

Start again. If this time he's out of position by lagging behind you, gently pull on the leash (a constant pull, not a tug!) and guide him into the heel position *while you continue walking.* Do not stop walking. As soon as he comes up into the heel position, relax the leash and praise him... but continue walking!

After he's been in the heel position for a few steps, give him a, "Take a break!"

Your goal is to get your Akita conditioned to walk alongside you in the heel position. The more time he spends in the heel position getting praise, the more time he'll want to spend in that position. Pretty soon it will be his regular position to be in while walking next to you-- after he hears you say, "Heel!"

If your Akita lags slightly behind you: Pull gently forward as you continue walking, but increase your speed. As your dog increases his speed (to avoid the tight leash and to match your walking speed) relax the leash and slow your pace, which will minimize the difference in position, so that you can praise him as he moves up into the heel position.

If you're still having trouble with lagging, there's no rule that says you can't palm a little cookie and pretend to glue your hand to your left hip. As your Akita comes up into the heel position to smell the cookie, reward him for coming into the heel position. Next, repeat the process while you're walking. Be sure to keep your hand glued to your left hip and only reward with the cookie when he is exactly in position.

After several repetitions you can phase out the cookie and your Akita will begin to understand where he should be when you drop your left hand down to your left hip and pull gently with the leash in your right hand.

If your Akita perpetually forges ahead, but is only slightly out of position: Pretend you are walking on a tight-rope and do a left-about turn. Hold the leash in your left hand and pull your left hand back, to get it out of the way and limit your dog's range of motion. As you do your left-about turn, cut into your dog, but stay as much on your imaginary tight rope as possible.

Bounce your knees up and down as if you were in your high school marching band.

Your Akita will want to avoid your knees and pull back into the heel position and look up at you. Praise him when he does!

If your Akita is forging far ahead: Simply do your right-about turn, just as you did with the attention-getter exercise. Remember to praise him when he comes up into position.

The trick to teaching the heel position is to make your Akita understand the contrast between being in position (and receiving all that wonderful praise and love!) versus being out of the heel position and feeling a mild irritant (a constant pull on the leash or a quick left-about-face change in direction).

It is a process of conditioning your Akita where to position himself. If you try to tug (a snap and release) if your dog is lagging, most likely he will lag more. This is when I would instead recommend one of the few times when it makes sense to lure your dog into position with food, just to help him understand where the position is.

Correcting Unwanted Behavior Such As Barking, Nipping, Jumping Up or Chewing

As I mentioned earlier, you'll need to have a training collar and either a leash or a tab on your Akita any time you're with him-- until he's 100%.

Once you've done the attention-getter exercise (above) your dog will be on a loose leash.

So, when your Akita barks, or jumps up, or does any other negative unwanted behavior, all you're going to do is: Say, "No!" and then reach down and grab the leash approximately one foot away from the snap and give a quick tug-and-release.

If your Akita keeps doing the behavior you've corrected him for, please revisit the Three Keys To Successful Behavior Modification (Timing, Consistency and Motivation) to troubleshoot which one of the three keys may not be working for you. Hint: For most people in most cases it's because your correction wasn't motivational or because you're not starting and finishing with slack in your leash. Make sure you're giving a quick snap.

Proofing

There are three phases your Akita will go through as he progresses through his training: The teaching phase, the reinforcement phase and the proofing phase.

The teaching phase is when your dog learns what the command means. The reinforcement phase is when you use repetition to drill the lesson into your Akita by repeating the exercise in a variety of different locations. The proofing phase is when you'll teach your dog to ignore all types of distractions.

It's okay to blend the proofing phase in with the reinforcement phase, once your Akita is showing you that he's fully understanding the exercise.

We'll usually start the proofing by asking our Akita to hold a position, for example: The place command. Then we'll move our body around the place board as if we were on the end of the big hand of a clock-- holding the leash with two hands so that we're ready to "zip" up the leash and correct him back onto the place board, should he decide to jump off.

Once your Akita will reliably stay in the (place position, in this case) is when we'll start with the proofing.

Grab a tennis ball and bounce it once. If he jumps off the place board, forget about the ball and correct him back onto the place board. Or into the sit position; the down-position; Etc...

Next, bounce the ball again. If your Akita stays on the place board, go back to him and praise him profusely. Then give him a, "take a break" command and let him play with the ball.

Rinse and repeat until you can walk all the way around him and continually bounce the ball without him breaking the command.

Then try the same thing with food.

Next, have a friend with a dog walk all the way around your Akita. If your dog breaks the position, you're going to simply correct him back into the place command. He needs to learn that his job is to stay put until you tell him, "take a break."

If your Akita keeps disobeying, return to the three keys to successful behavior modification (timing, consistency and motivation) to figure out which of the keys is not working for you, and then make the appropriate adjustments.

Next, have a friend grab the neighbor's cat and walk around your dog. A leaf blower. A bicycle. Anything you can think of to tempt your dog. When your dog makes the right decision, praise him profusely.

Pretty soon you'll get to a point where you simply will not be able to find a distraction that makes your dog break the command. And that's how you proof a Akita.

You should attempt to proof your Akita to be responsive with all commands, and that includes the, "Come" command. Just keep coming up with creative distractions and every time your dog makes the right decision, be sure to praise him. When he makes the wrong decision, correct him and make him come all the way back to you, anyway. Then immediately put him in front of the same distraction again to see if he learned. When he does it correctly? You guessed it... praise him for making the right choice.

Why Crate Training
Your Akita Is Important

Every top professional dog trainer I've ever met uses a kennel crate to keep their Akitas safe and secure when they're not around.

Plain and simple, you'll need to confine your Akita to either a crate (or a kennel run) when you cannot keep one eye on him and one eye on whatever else you're doing... until your dog proves himself to be 100% reliable.

The crate you choose should be secure and of a quality build. We recommend the plastic airline approved crates as these tend to be much more durable and less easy for a dog to escape from.

The idea behind using a crate is similar to a crib or a play pen for a child. It's not to be used as punishment but rather as your Akita's "safe place" where he can relax and know that he won't be bothered.

And you can rest assured knowing that since he's confined, he won't get into trouble and develop bad habits while you're busy doing something else.

Akitas are den animals and they derive a sense of confidence and well being from being in a small, enclosed space. Pay attention to your dog and you'll probably find that he naturally gravitates toward being under your desk or in a place where his back side is protected.

Confine your Akita in a crate at night while you're sleeping and during the day when you need to leave him alone.

A general rule of thumb is that for the first seven months of your dog's life he can be expected to stay in the crate *during the day* a maximum of one hour for every month of age... plus one. For example: If your dog is three months-old, then it's reasonable to expect him to stay in the crate for four hours. If your dog is six months-old, then he can stay in the crate for seven hours.

(Although we recommend only keeping him in the crate for that many hours over night, not during the day).

If you work away from the house, you may need to either find a way to bring your dog (and his crate) to work with you. Or enlist the help of a neighbor or pet sitter who can stop by your house in the middle of the day and give your dog a potty break and some exercise.

"But isn't confining my Akita during the day when I'm not home too much confinement?"

No. The fact of the matter is: Your Akita spends on average 80% of any 24 hour period either sleeping or resting. He's simply not running around the house or yard all day. So, by confining him in his crate, we're just limiting his freedom (and his opportunity to develop bad habits) for now.

Later, when your Akita is older and able to handle the responsibility, you won't need to crate him when you're not around.

As a general rule of thumb: We will crate a puppy anytime we're not there to supervise until approximately one year to 1.5 years of age. When we adopt an older dog, we'll typically crate him for the first six months to one year that we've had him. This gives us enough time to supervise and spy on him to make sure he's not sneaking into another room and learning bad behaviors, be it chewing on baseboard or jumping on furniture.